THE LITTLE
BLACK BOOK OF

SEX

• A Lover's Guide to Doing It Right •

RUTH CULLEN

ILLUSTRATED BY KERREN BARBAS

PETER PAUPER PRESS, INC.
WHITE PLAINS, NEW YORK

FOR MY SMART-N-SEXY SISTER, DR. NO

SPECIAL THANKS TO MY LIFELONG PALS,
THE RENEGADE FROGS,
FOR THEIR EXPERTISE AND
FIELD RESEARCH

Designed by Heather Zschock

Illustrations copyright © 2004 Kerren Barbas

Copyright © 2004
Pete Pauper Press, Inc.
202 Mamaroneck Avenue
White Plains, NY 10601

ISBN 978-0-88088-570-6
Printed in Hong Kong
14 13 12 11 10 9 8

Visit us at www.peterpauper.com

THE LITTLE
BLACK BOOK OF
SEX

CONTENTS

INTRODUCTION

We all want it. In fact, we want it so badly we will do just about anything to get it. And when we do get it, we just want more of it . . . and more, and more, and more.

But having sex does not an expert make.

There's a world of information beyond the birds and bees and storks your mother might have told you about. Unfortunately, many important questions about physical and emotional intimacy go unanswered because there is simply no one to ask.

Until now, that is.

The Little Black Book of Sex is your go-to guide for the bottom line, tell-it-to-me-straight truth about sex. The stuff your mother didn't know how to begin to explain.

You'll find answers to your questions and get specific how to's, dos and don'ts, and why nots. You'll even learn some fascinating facts that'll really impress your friends (and loved ones).

Best of all, you'll discover that nothing you read in this book will taint your soul for all eternity, make you go blind, or give you a rash. (Well, maybe just a temporary flush.) In fact, you might just "see the light" about sex, and learn facts and tips that may well save your soul.

Have fun and play it safe!
R. C.

sex

Sex appeal is 50% what you've
got and 50% what people
think you've got.

—*Sophia Loren*

THE INS AND OUTS

FIFTEEN MINUTES. That's the average length of time most heterosexual couples spend having sex—though one could say that taking anywhere from 10 minutes to an hour is "normal."

The rest of the time we just obsess about it. We spend hours each day fantasizing about it, scheming ways to get it, crying because of it (or the lack of it), and studying both the art (that is, expression and interpretation) and science (mostly biology, chemistry, and physics) of sex. But most of us probably actually "do it" only a few times a week.

Sex in real life is far more complicated and a lot more messy than the sex we see projected from newsstands, computer screens, and TVs—especially the stuff of "reality shows" that reveals far more Hollywood gloss than true grit.

And despite an omnipresence of sexual images and innuendo in our culture, when it comes right down to it, there's nothing more personal, more private, and more mysterious than sex between consenting adults (unless we're talking about the sex you have with yourself).

There's also nothing more misunderstood—judging from the latest figures on HIV and other sexually transmitted diseases, teen pregnancy, and the popularity of Dr. Phil.

Only after we shed some of the many conflicting emotions we feel about sex—the guilt, fear, and embarrassment—will we begin to understand it. And only then will we realize that acquiring sexual knowledge does not make one perverted or promiscuous; it simply makes one smart.

So let us wrap our arms around this thing called sex by first defining what it is.

THE NAKED TRUTH

WHEN WE'RE TALKING ABOUT "HAVING SEX," we're generally referring to sexual intercourse. Technically, that's copulation, coitus, or sexual relations (if you happen to be a president), and, less technically, mattress dancing, bonking, or shagging (if you happen to be British).

Whatever you call it, the sex you read about in this book primarily involves the insertion of a penis into a vagina, unless, of course, we're specifically discussing other body parts and the intriguing ways they can connect.

Sex also refers to the structural and functional differences between males and females of any given species. We'll take off our collective pants and have a good look at male and female genitalia— namely, penises, vulvas, and

other tickly parts.

Before we do, though, let's examine a few basic questions about sex. Like, why do we do it? What compels us to press the flesh of our most private of areas? What force drives us to expose our thongs, dirty dance on table tops, and wear jewelry where the sun don't shine?

THE URGE TO MERGE

Scientists have long studied these very questions.

Hours upon hours of tedious research in laboratories, singles hotspots, and hotel bars leads to the general conclusion that sexual energy brings us together—quite literally, in fact.

We humans are innately driven to procreate, to ensure propagation of the species by spreading our genetic seeds throughout the land. We are also driven to couple, to share our lives with another person in a meaningful, satisfying, loving way.

As such, we do whatever we think it takes to make ourselves attractive to someone else. We ratchet up our sex appeal with sense appeal; that is, we try to look inviting, sound intriguing, smell invigorating, feel touchable, and taste absolutely scrumptious.

> ### Qualities of women that attract men the most (in order)
>
> PERSONALITY
> BEAUTY
> SENSE OF HUMOR
> SMILE
> INTELLIGENCE

Sometimes we make bold public displays, such as singing "Sexual Healing" to our dates on karaoke night. At other times, we pay surgeons gobs of money to sculpt our bodies into idealistic visions of loveliness.

However, our efforts aside, experts believe that natural body chemicals called pheromones play the leading role in determining whom we find attractive and with whom we will ultimately mate. Like the scent of freshly baked bread that lures us into the bakery, pheromones may explain why we are drawn to people very different from ourselves (read: opposites attract), and why we occasionally act upon our sudden feelings of passion (read: one night stands).

Pheromones or not, the powerful desire to couple is sometimes simply that: a powerful desire to couple. Forget procreation, love, and happily ever after, people have sex because it's fun and it feels good—not to mention other reasons like stress release, lust, conquest, and just plain old horniness.

Your Sexual ID

SEXUALLY SPEAKING, how we act does not necessarily indicate who we are. Married with kids and living in the 'burbs doesn't make you straight, just as girl-on-girl kissing on national TV doesn't make you gay (just really, really hip).

It's whom we desire, fantasize about, and crave that dictates who we really are.

Luckily, the vast majority of us have known since childhood which way we lean. We discovered our bodies' reactions to certain stimuli (say, Victoria's Secret catalogs or the UPS man) and never looked back.

But lines of sexual preference are not always so neatly drawn.

Through the years, researchers, most notably the late Dr. Alfred C. Kinsey, have identified a spectrum of human sexual behavior that falls anywhere between exclusive heterosexuality and exclusive homosexuality. For those caught in the middle, sexuality can be pretty tricky to say the least.

The relatively new term "metrosexual" refers to straight men living primarily in urban areas who devote much time and energy to their style and appearance. Metrosexuals openly embrace designer trends and male beauty products, never shying away from a good hair gel, facial moisturizer, or manicure.

Regardless of who, or what (as the case may be) floats your boat, the best way to embrace your sexual identity is to love and accept yourself for who you are.

AFTER THE LOVING

The temporary thrill of delirious, satisfying sex pales in comparison to the pain and suffering that can come with the territory.

Nothing kills the morning after like the fear of an unwanted pregnancy or the reality of some disgusting sexually transmitted disease. Only condoms can prevent HIV; condoms plus some other form of birth control prevent babies. Do yourself a favor and protect yourself against the possible unwanted consequences of sex. (Read more about STDs and contraceptives on pages 123-131.)

Heartache, on the other hand, occurs when you least expect it and is not entirely preventable. You see, many people (especially women) confuse physical intimacy with emotional intimacy, mistakenly believing that sexual closeness will spark an emotional

connection leading to a long-term, committed relationship. Not so.

Similarly, hearts can break when relationships go south, and this happens for all kinds
of reasons (e.g., she sleeps with your best
friend; he sleeps with your mother). For a
more complete listing on how love goes
wrong, just listen to any country music sta-
tion for about an hour.

READY, SET, GET IT ON

Before you decide to activate your sex life, for the first time ever or the first time today, it's critical that you ask yourself a few questions:

Emotional, Physical, and Intellectual Readiness for Sex—A Quiz

YES NO

○ ○ 1. Do I really want to have sex? (If NO, skip to Answer Key.)

○ ○ 2. Do I really want to make a baby? (If YES, skip to question 4.)

○ ○ 3. Have I personally taken care of contraceptive needs?

○ ○ 4. Have I protected myself against HIV and other STDs? (If YES, skip to question 6.)

YES   NO

○   ○   5. Have I envisioned my parents' faces when they learn about my genital warts, HIV-positive status, and their newest grandchild (perhaps all at the same time)?

○   ○   6. Am I sober? (If YES, skip to question 8.)

○   ○   7. Am I so plastered that I don't know where I am or why I'm naked with a lamp shade on my head? (If NO, skip to question 8.)

○   ○   8. Do I care if I am having sex for love (e.g., Mr./Ms. Right) or lust (e.g., Mr./Ms. Right Now)?

○   ○   9. Might having sex with this person get me promoted, fired, or arrested?

○   ○   10. Do I know where to obtain a restraining order and how they work?

Answer Key

Look, answers are overrated. And you already have them all, don't you?

You, like all smart people, gather as much information as you can to keep yourself safe, satisfied, and in control of whatever transpires when clothes come off.

In matters of sex, smart people ultimately do what feels right for them.

That said, the following friendly reminders may help keep you in check:

Only *you* will know when you're ready to have sex. Until then, keep your pants on and find other ways to have fun. Bowling, for example.

Don't worry. Be happy. Do this by practicing safe sex using condoms and contraceptives.

Don't let alcohol or anything else serve as a convenient excuse for your actions, particularly if they include performing a strip tease at the office holiday party or assaulting the family pet.

Keep your sexpectations in check. Namely, get a grip on what you expect from your partner after the sex is done (e.g., tender canoodling, follow-up phone call, big wad of cash).

It takes a long time to get to know someone, and sometimes you don't realize what an absolute, lunatic freak you're with until after you've shared a bed. That's when things can get downright scary (think: Glenn Close's character in the movie *Fatal Attraction*). So before you hop in the sack with someone you just met, seriously consider not only your potential risk and vulnerability, but especially your pet rabbit's.

I'll show you mine if you show me yours.

It's better to be looked over
than overlooked.

—*Mae West*

A healthy body image is the sexiest thing you can bring to bed.

Granted, healthy, well-toned bodies with ample appendages can make for delightfully fun and creative sex. (By the way, men tend to concentrate on breasts and butts, while women are most attracted to chests and mouths.)

But bodies attached to minds that perceive them as inadequate or unattractive— regardless of their shape or size—add a level  of self-consciousness that really puts a damper on sex.

Only after we come to understand and appreciate our bodies and how they work can we freely and confidently share their splendors with someone else.

MANLY BITS

WHO'S THE MOST POPULAR FISH IN THE SEA? No, it's not that talking tuna character; it's the blue whale. Here's a visual for you: ten foot long penis, one foot in diameter.

And the king of the jungle may well be the African elephant, so well-endowed and talented that he can use his six-footer to scratch his own belly.

It's no wonder men are so hung up on their packages—and not simply regarding matters of size or dexterity. A man's crotch area is his command center, his center of gravity. A quick ball check or penis squeeze lets him know that everything's going to be OK.

Unlike other digital manipulations of the male genitals, the crotch grab may simply be a loving, protective gesture toward the family jewels.

PENISES AND SNOWFLAKES

So uniquely different, and yet so alike.

With the possible exception of clones and, say, identical twins, no two penises are exactly the same. Some are short and stubby, like kosher dill pickles, while others hang lean and long, like, since we're talking cucumbers, the English Hothouse variety.

The average penis measures up at around six inches long.

In the flaccid, un-aroused state, penises generally hang in a southerly direction, leaning to the east or west at the discretion of the testicles. (If the right testicle hangs lower than the left, for example, the penis will do a right face, so to speak.) The angle of the dangle sharply changes, however, when the penis becomes erect during heightened states of arousal. As the penis becomes engorged with blood, the erection climbs northward until it reaches its peak—usually at an angle between 45-80 degrees. (90 degrees would be straight out.)

Penises come in two main styles: circumcised and uncircumcised. The majority of the world's male population is uncircumcised; that is, penises are left untouched in their natural "dressed" state with a foreskin covering the head, or glans, of the penis.

Circumcision, the practice of surgically removing the foreskin from the penis, has been around for centuries and remains popular today, despite an increasing amount of controversy about its pros and cons. Aside from religious reasons, those in favor of the snip argue that the procedure results in fewer hygiene-related infections and ailments caused by an accumulation of smegma (white, cheesy stuff) under the foreskin. Anti-circumcision types disagree, claiming that the foreskin plays an important role in protecting the ultra-sensitive tip of the penis and enhancing sensation during sexual stimulation. They also refute the foreskin's causal relationship with infections and other ailments, instead blaming that familiar culprit: poor hygiene.

Whatever the style, penises play a most important role in human sexuality and, indeed, the flow of everyday business.

PLANTING AND WATERING

A man's package consists of one (1) penis and two (2) testicles. One twig, two berries.

A multi-purpose organ, the penis is biologically engineered to rid the body of urine and plant seeds for future generations—just not at the same time.

The watering part's relatively straightforward. The urethra, or pee tube, runs from the bladder all the way down the center of the penile shaft, ending at the tip, or glans, of the penis. When enough urine collects in the bladder, man and his penis take the cue and do their thing.

The planting part is a bit more complicated. Males deposit their genetic seeds in females during sexual intercourse, when they

 ejaculate semen containing millions of tiny sex cells called sperm into a woman's vagina. Once inside, sperm wriggle their way upstream in search of the female's egg. Fertilization occurs when sperm penetrates egg, thus combining the male and female halves of the genetic equation.

Because these male sex cells play such a vital reproductive role, nature created special housing and production facilities just for them: the testicles.

The testicles hang outside the body below the shaft of the penis encased in a wrinkled bag of skin called the scrotal sac. Since men commonly refer to their testicles as "nuts" or "balls," it's not surprising that some women mistakenly believe that testicles resemble two distinct balls of flesh hanging beneath the penis. This is not the case, though the testicles do move about freely as two separate entities within a single pouch of skin.

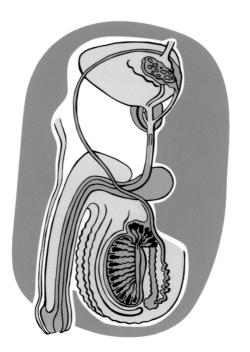

Each day, the testicles produce millions of sperm cells and nearly all of the male hormone testosterone.

To grow healthy, fast swimming sperm, the testicles must maintain a temperature slightly below body temperature. That's why ball sacs shrivel up against the body when it's cold, or swing in the breeze when it's warm. It also explains why sperm counts plummet when men spend too much time in extra hot Jacuzzis or in really tight underwear. Other factors, like testicular trauma, can impact sperm production and cause infertility problems later in life.

Testosterone makes men out of boys, giving them deep voices, strong upper bodies, and lots and lots of hair. In some cases, testosterone makes men out of women, but that's another story. Testosterone levels also affect sex drive in both men and women, most evident in people with too much (e.g., players in the National Basketball Association) or too little (e.g., members of the National Library Association).

HARD WOOD

LIKE THOSE HOTDOGS AT THE BALL PARK THAT PLUMP WHEN YOU COOK THEM,

 penises have a remarkable ability to grow in size and firmness when things heat up (in the bedroom, not in the kitchen). Actually, erections occur spontaneously for most men when they are stimulated by touch, sensation, or an intriguing visual. Even baby boys commonly experience erections while they sleep, a fact some scientists believe is nature's way of ensuring adequate oxygen levels in the penis.

While men welcome their erections at all the right times—such as when duty (or booty) calls—unwanted wood can be inconvenient and downright embarrassing, especially if it happens during a public speaking event or the church bake sale.

So how does the penis transform itself from limp to firm to rock solid hard?

Well, if you've ever inflated a balloon, you know how quickly an object can mutate from one form to another. And if you've ever over-inflated something, like a rubber ball or a bicycle tire, you know how firm a malleable object can become.

The penis achieves a similar state when blood, not air, rushes into the corpora cavernosa, the two main tubes of erectile tissue on either side of the penile shaft. Once completely engorged with blood, the penis feels rigid and firm to the touch—almost like a bone (and thus the term "boner").

If ignored, most erections will gradually subside until the penis returns to its relaxed, flaccid state.

If further stimulated, particularly on the

ultra-sensitive underside of the head called the frenulum, erections may lead to heightened states of sexual arousal, culminating in the pleasurable, sexual release of orgasm and, more times than not, the ejaculation of semen from the tip of the penis.

Penises and Cream

Much like some country line dances, ejaculation is a two-step process.

First, the Cowper's glands release a pre-ejaculatory fluid containing some sperm. Just prior to ejaculation, this clear fluid is present at the tip of the penis.

Next, sperm work their way through the epididymis and vas deferens to mix with fluid from the seminal vesicles and prostate gland. The milky white fluid that results is called semen, which then travels down the urethra before its emission from the tip of the penis.

Unlike our friend the blue whale, who ejaculates about five gallons at a time, the average man produces about one teaspoon of the white stuff each time he spouts.

In sexual encounters, the timing of ejaculation can be a source of pride for some, or complete and utter frustration for others. Although they are two separate and distinct functions, ejaculation and orgasm typically happen simultaneously. For many men, focusing on a partner's orgasm prior to their own makes for mutually satisfying sex.

However, many men struggle with premature ejaculation, leaving them and their partners feeling as if the party has ended before it's begun. On the flip side, retarded ejaculation, or the inability to ejaculate when desired or at all, can ultimately cause great frustration and anxiety. Luckily, help for these and other sexual problems may be as close as your urologist's office, so it's always best to consult the experts whenever concerns arise.

womanly wares

Being a sex symbol has to do
with an attitude, not looks.
Most men think it's looks, most
women know otherwise.

—*Kathleen Turner*

Females have always had a complicated relationship with their bodies.

It usually starts around puberty, when womanhood waves her estrogen wand and bestows girls with breasts, hips, and lots of small, curly hairs. Then, of course, there's the discovery that each month brings with it a healthy dose of pain, bloating, and blood.

Where girls were once carefree and oblivious, they're now as teens often obsessive and compulsive, dissecting their bodies like frogs in science class, and always concluding that some part or another is too big, too small, or just plain ugly.

But they're not the only ones critiquing their bodies. Suddenly, it seems, the world views them differently. Boys take notice, and even grown men stare just a second too long.

For the lucky ones, insecurity and unease give way to a growing sense of power—an

acceptance and appreciation of their bodies that translates into self-confidence and, most certainly, sex appeal. They learn to see themselves as the luscious, curvaceous goddesses they are.

Others can sink into an abyss of self loathing, confusing body image with self worth and seeking remedies in cosmetics and plastic surgery instead of psychiatry.

For all women, however, the road to enlightenment is paved with, well, knowledge. And for many women, self knowledge is seriously lacking. They simply don't know much about the mechanics of the female organs, or, for that matter, what to call them.

VULVAS, HOOSIES, AND WHATCHAMACALLITS

Experts advise parents to teach their children the proper names for body parts: "This is your nose, these are your toes, this is your vulva . . . "

But for reasons known only to them, many parents seem unable or unwilling to present the straight facts. Girls walk away from childhood armed with euphemisms (e.g., thingy, privates, down there) but short on facts.

In the end, it takes a while for women to get to know their Melvins, or, rather, vulvas. Whereas men have had a close, personal relationship with their penises since birth, many women reach adulthood without ever standing over a mirror and having a good look.

READING BETWEEN THE LIPS

Women have a lot of lips. Three sets to be exact, if you include the ones on the face.

But forget about facial, lipstick lips for a moment, and scan down to a woman's crotch.

The external female genitalia are known as the vulva—not the vagina, which is internal—and consist of several parts.

The mons pubis is the fleshy, often hair-covered mound of skin covering the pubic bone. Directly beneath the mons pubis lie two outer folds of skin known as the labia majora. These external lips tend to be hairy and less sensitive than the labia minora, the delicate inner lips they conceal.

Parting the outer lips just below the

mons pubis reveals a hood of skin concealing a little nubbin called the clitoris. When sexually aroused, female tissues swell with blood and the tip of the clitoris becomes erect, much like a male's penis does. In fact, both male and female genitals look exactly the same during the first weeks of embryonic development, before they go their separate ways.

Due south of the clitoris lies the urethral opening, the end of the line for the urethra, which carries urine from the bladder out of the body.

And below the urethral opening is the vaginal opening, the entrance into the vagina and the gateway to the internal, female reproductive organs.

SLIPPERY WHEN WET

To begin to understand the mystery that shrouds the vagina, one must first get comfortable saying the word.

Repeat the following three times: Carolina. Aunt Jemima. Hands off that's mine-ah. Vagina.

All right. That's much better.

The tunnel of love that is the vagina consists of a four-inch-deep expandable cavity lined by smooth, muscular walls.

When a woman is sexually aroused, two small glands near the vaginal opening called Bartholin's glands secrete a clear, lubricating fluid that slicks the vaginal opening and surrounding area.

Blood swells tissues outside and within the vagina, a process called tumescence, and lubricating droplets "sweat" off vaginal walls providing a slippery slope for penises or other penetrating objects.

The female hormone estrogen directly affects vaginal lubrication, so when estrogen levels surge, vaginal wetness occurs, regardless of whether or not a woman is sexually aroused. On the other hand, when estrogen levels drop during menopause, many women experience vaginal dryness, a condition easily remedied with any number of over-the-counter lubrications.

Vaginas are self-cleaning organs, and, as such, do not respond well to products with heavy cleansers or perfumes. Any normal, white discharge that collects can be rinsed away with ordinary soap and water. However, anything out of the ordinary—colorful discharge, foul odors, painful sores—requires the immediate attention of a gynecologist.

CRIMSON TIDE

BY FAR THE MOST VALUABLE FEMALE PLAYERS IN THE GAME OF REPRODUCTION ARE THE OVARIES, the two peach pit-sized organs that house a woman's lifetime supply of eggs—over 200,000 in total. Each egg contains the female half of the genetic equation.

About every 28 days or so, little fluid-filled sacs in the ovaries called follicles release an egg in a process called ovulation. The tiny egg travels down the fallopian tubes and into the uterus, a muscular organ lined by tissue called endometrium.

If the egg is unfertilized, the body sheds both the egg and the endometrial lining about two weeks later during a process called menstruation. Menstrual blood passes out of the uterus by way of the cervix, then exits the body through the vagina.

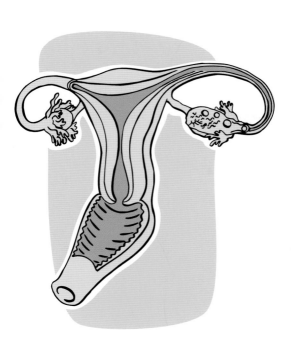

However, if just one little sperm cell wiggled its way into a woman's vagina in the two-to-seven day period around ovulation, egg and sperm might meet, mingle, and live happily ever after as one (baby, that is).

Here's why. In the two weeks before ovulation, clear, watery mucus produced by the  cervix creates excellent swimming conditions for sperm. From the vagina, sperm can ride the wave of cervical mucus through the cervix, uterus, and into the fallopian tubes. A female's egg remains fertile for three days, and if sperm penetrates egg, the resulting embryo will settle in the uterus, attached to the endometrial lining, where it will grow and grow and grow. About nine months later, it will squeeze through the female's ever-expandable vagina in search of loving parents who will provide for its every need.

For some women, menstruation is more than just shedding blood. Those who suffer from pre-menstrual syndrome (PMS) may experience sudden mood swings or food cravings. As of yet, PMS has not been scientifically proven, but sharing this fact with a pre-menstrual woman may likely result in additional bloodshed.

And during menstruation, many women experience some discomfort caused by bloating and cramping. In addition to over-the-counter remedies, the sexual release of orgasm may help alleviate these symptoms. For this reason and more, sex during the menstrual period can be as pleasurable as, if not more than, any other time. Of course, due to the easy transmission of HIV and other nasty germs through blood and body fluids, it's especially important at this time that men wear condoms. It's also advisable to plan ahead for a potentially messy scenario, unless you don't mind the look of slaughtered chickens on your bed.

THE PEARL IN THE OYSTER

Of all the intriguing parts in a woman's nether region, only one provides nothing but pleasure.

The clitoris, unlike its distant, multi-purpose relative, the penis, exists for the sole purpose of giving pleasure—pure, unadulterated, overwhelming ecstasy.

The right combination of touches applied to the clitoris will envelop a woman's entire body with delicious tingling sensations that rise and fall over and over and over again.

Because, well, that's just what clitorises do.

MELONS AND MOSQUITO BITES

Just the sight of a woman's breast can trigger an involuntary reaction in a man's pants.

Go figure, but breasts have stimulated libidos for as long as they've been around—and that's a long time.

Big, small, or in between, breasts make great play things. It's always fun to watch nipples become erect from the slightest touch or softest breeze. And nuzzling, kissing, caressing, and squeezing breasts can bring immense satisfaction to everyone involved.

In fact, some women feel a definite connection between their nipples and vulvas—a  connection strengthened by the fact that nipple stimulation during pregnancy and nursing can cause the uterus to contract.

But beware: breasts do not always welcome touch. At certain times during a woman's menstrual cycle, a hands-off or proceed-with-caution policy works best since some women experience particularly sensitive or painful breasts. Squeezing tender breasts may leave the squeezer with a black eye.

That said, the best policy for breast and all sexual play involves paying close attention to the woman behind the parts, and basing actions accordingly.

rounding the phases

Sex is hardly ever just about sex.

—*Shirley MacLaine*

THE "DING-A-LING-A-LING" OF THE ICE-CREAM TRUCK SETS OFF A DISTINCT CHAIN OF EVENTS: children shriek with excitement ("Ice-cream maaaan!!!"); beg, borrow, or steal money from the nearest adult; then sprint onto the street, jumping and waving as if, at long last, the rescue plane has arrived at their desert island.

Similarly, sexual stimulation of the human body generates a consistent pattern of responses.

So said Drs. William Masters and Virginia Johnson, two pioneers in the field of sex research who spent years in the laboratory observing thousands of couples having sex.

 They didn't watch just for the fun of it (well, maybe just a little); they wired their subjects and exhaustively studied, monitored, and measured every-

thing from breathing to blood pressure, sweat to semen.

In the end, they identified four distinct phases of the human sexual response cycle.

CLIMBING THE MOUNTAIN

During the Excitement Phase, bodies heat up as they become increasingly more aroused.

In both men and women, a process called vasocongestion causes blood to swell tissues in the penis, clitoris, vaginal lips, and breasts. The penis, clitoris, and nipples become erect, and breast tissues swell up to 20% in size.

Muscles in the arms and legs start to feel tense.

Vaginal walls begin to produce lubrication, and functions like blood pressure and breathing rate increase.

Some people can't hide their excitement

and break out in rash—a "sex flush" that usually appears around the rib cage before spreading to the chest.

One key difference between the sexes in this phase involves timing. Namely, men get aroused far more quickly than women do, making foreplay more a necessity than a luxury. (Read more about foreplay starting on page 67.)

KEEPING IT REAL

Think of the Plateau (second) Phase as the Excitement Phase cranked up a few degrees.

Excitement levels increase before leveling off to a period of prolonged, pleasurable sensations.

Masters and Johnson observed two main changes in males during the Plateau Phase: first, a clear, pre-ejaculatory fluid released by the Cowper's glands appears at the head of the penis; and second, the testicles enlarge and contract into the body.

Many couples enjoy the lingering sensations of heightened arousal, and attempt to draw out this phase as long as possible. Followers of Tantra, which originated from Taoist and Buddhist philosophies, may spend hours delighting in the splendors of this phase.

THE BIG O

The Orgasm Phase involves a lot of oohs and aahs, and sometimes grunts, yelps, and screams, as bodies succumb to the pleasurable waves of sensation climax brings during sexual release.

It may look painful, but when bodies contort, contract, and spasm during orgasm, it's all good. Very, very good.

Vital signs peak with every gasped breath, and hearts pump stronger and faster. The genitals, the source of much of the pleasurable sensation orgasm brings, experience strong contractions that gradually subside. Even toes curl.

When men ejaculate, they first experience a feeling of inevitability, a sensation caused when seminal liquids are squeezed into the urethra. This produces a feeling of imminent orgasm only a few seconds beforehand. Then, a series of contractions forces semen out of the penis in squirts. Generally speaking, the larger the volume of semen ejaculated, the more intense the orgasm.

AAHS AND SNORES

Men experience sudden, obvious changes during the Resolution Phase immediately following orgasm.

Mere seconds after ejaculation, erections melt away and bodies return to their normal, pre-excited states. This quick cool-down, coupled with the sense of relaxation that comes after satisfying sexual release, leaves many men snoring between the sheets. Men also have a refractory period, a necessary time-out before they can get erections and start the sexual response cycle all over again. This refractory period increases as men age.

On the other hand, women, like irons, take longer to heat up and cool down. In fact, because women have the ability to experience multiple, successive orgasms, they may welcome additional touches after orgasm.

An important part of the Resolution Phase for both men and women involves afterplay, the various activities that take place after intercourse which can include everything from tender, intimate pillow talk to ordering Chinese take-out. These moments after passionate sex can be a special time of reconnecting for couples, even if it means just mutually basking in the afterglow of great sex and falling asleep in each other's arms.

come-ons and turn-ons

Delightful Euphemisms for Sex

Checking Her Oil
Parking the Pink Cadillac
Horizontal Jogging
Assault with a Friendly Weapon
Burying the Bone
Playing Hide the Salami
Interior Decorating

Ask any man what really turns him on, and chances are he'll say "naked boobies."

Ask any woman what gets her in the mood, and she'll likely rattle off a well-composed list: "flowers, chocolates, dinner by candlelight, anything from Cartier." If she's married, something to the effect of "when my husband does the dishes" will undoubtedly top her list.

The factors that pique sexual interest vary by person and run the gamut of possibilities—from body parts to body language, from aromas to sounds to tastes.

For centuries, people have experimented with aphrodisiacs—specific foods or substances thought to stimulate sexual desire and enhance romance in one way or another. One of the most popular aphrodisiacs, alcohol, when consumed in moderation, may indeed help some people limber up and lose their inhibitions. But drinking too much can have the opposite effect, limiting one's physical ability to have sex and extinguishing any romantic flames with all the wrong body fluids.

By far the best way to turn on your partner is to tune in to him or her. Engage in psychological foreplay by using your most sexual organ—your brain. Pay attention to your partner's verbal and nonverbal cues, and respond in ways that leave your partner hungering for more.

DANGLING THE CARROT

Your mother was right: less is more.

Sensual hints, like a delicate lace camisole that peeks out from beneath a silk blouse, or a tiny dab of cologne on the neck, prove far more effective than transparent, over-the-top actions. You don't have to writhe and thrust half naked in a pool of mud to capture someone's attention.

One way to attract the right moths to your flame is to seduce them with your eyes. Lingering or fleeting glances can say far more than the average booty shake.

People who stand tall and smile exude confidence, and confidence is sexy. Other body language, like wetting your lips before you speak, or casually touching someone's hand to emphasize a point, can send messages that intrigue as they inspire—particularly if combined with a look that says, "I mean everything I say."

SLIPPING THE TONGUE

SOMETIMES WHAT GOES IN AND OUT OF OUR MOUTHS CAN MAKE OR BREAK A DATE.

For example:

Say, "Sure, who doesn't love foot-long hot dogs?"

Never Say: "I got your foot-long hot dog right here, babe. Heh, heh."

When executed correctly in the right circumstances, sexual innuendo, or the use of intentionally ambiguous words or phrases that conjure sexual images, can succeed in raising a few eyebrows and igniting sparks down below.

On the flip side, rather than beating around the bush, sometimes the best approach is to head straight for it.

Indeed, some people get very aroused

when a partner tells them exactly what they want. Since men usually initiate sex, they especially enjoy the reversal of roles when women control the action and take matters into their own hands.

Explicitly naughty talk, or dirty XXX-rated chit chat, is best shared between couples who know each other really well. Otherwise, you risk bodily injury when your offended partner hurls objects in your direction.

And while you might feel safer by talking dirty on computer screens or telephones, consider the following: caller ID; un-erasable hard drives; your company's information services department; sexual harassment laws and policies; and your neighbor's baby monitor that also monitors conversations you have on your cordless phone.

STIRRING THE POT

When we're talking turn-ons, some of the most popular are also some of the most obvious.

Take good personal hygiene, for example. No one wants to get up close and personal with someone who smells bad, looks crusty, and tastes even worse—conditions that arise from too much perfume, aftershave, make-up, body glitter, body lotion, mousse, gel, or hair spray. So it's no surprise that clever men and women incorporate bathing into sex, figuring they can ensure the cleanliness of their partners by luring them into showers and bath tubs with the promise of naked, soapy friction.

 Vivid or implied sexual images can excite powerful responses in the visually stimulated male population (and in some part of the female population), a fact that women and purveyors of pornography know full well. Thus, many couples preview their own carnal pleasures by viewing others pursuing the same. Occasionally, this involves the

use of a high quality telescope perched at the window, but usually it just means renting a few porn flicks from the local video store.

Other popular turn-ons include: lingerie; absence of lingerie; the Brazilian bikini wax (think: bald is beautiful); 5 o'clock shadows (or not); hair on chests (or not); sex in strange places (think: kitchen pantry); fear of being discovered while having sex (hopefully not by law enforcement); use of sex toys; role play; fantasy play; unusual body piercings; and large, inflatable rubber chicken suits.

Just kidding about that last one.

Inner traits like kindness, trustworthiness, dependability, and ambition by far surpass the temporary thrills of, say, lipstick and heels (on him that is). And the telltale signs of wealth and power undeniably attract people looking to feel a sense of their own.

But the biggest turn-on of all, beyond diamonds, garter belts, and even vibrators, is love—the tender, passionate affection for someone else that makes your heart go pitter pat and sends tingling shivers down your spine.

for playas only

Common Sex Myths

Shoe size indicates penis size.
Masturbation will make you blind.
Women can't get pregnant during their periods.
Bigger is always better.
Men can't achieve orgasm without ejaculating.

Foreplay doesn't just apply to sex.

We lovingly play with our food, using fingers, lips, and tongues to derive immense sensual pleasure from the shapes, colors, and textures of nature's bounty: succulent peaches; ripe, red tomatoes; bold, green zucchinis. Hours spent in the kitchen while we prep, stir, and baste tantalize and delight us long before we ever take a bite.

With the right attitude, the process of pursuing just about any goal—climbing a mountain, driving across country, completing the seventh grade—becomes more personally fulfilling with every peak, valley, or roadblock.

Because it's the journey, man, not the destination.

Foreplay includes everything you say and do before genitals physically connect. It's the midday phone call to say, "I'm getting hot just hearing your voice." It's the loving gaze, the clasp of intertwined fingers, and the first, tender brush of lips.

More than anything, foreplay involves play, lots of focused, whimsical, exploratory play that makes pleasure linger and last.

E-ZONES AND G-SPOTS

THE ENTIRE BODY CAN BE CONSIDERED AN EROGENOUS ZONE, although specific key areas have extra nerve endings making them acutely sensitive to sexual stimulation.

In either sex, some of the most sensitive body parts include the mouth, tongue, ears, nipples, perineum, buttocks, and anus. Some people love toes, and the fondling of their partner's toes or their own may give them a rise. Wherever your touch takes you, focus your attention on your partner's reactions, and vary your caresses, licks, breaths, and squeezes accordingly.

In men, the penis responds immediately and obviously to touch, especially on the ultra

 sensitive glans (head) and the frenulum, the skin on the underside of the head. The oft-neglected scrotum responds well to gentle to

medium-firm touch, though too much pressure will cause discomfort.

A popular technique for stimulating the penis involves grasping the shaft with one hand and applying strokes of various speeds and pressures in an up and down motion. The other hand may be used to cup and gently squeeze the scrotum, or to apply pressure at the base of the penis.

Another highly erogenous zone for many men lies just inside the back door. The prostate gland sits below the bladder at the (internal) base of the penis. Applying pressure to the prostate, either by pressing on the perineum or inserting a lubricated, gloved finger into the rectum and pressing down, stimulates numerous nerve endings leading to the penis. It's not called the male G-spot for nothing.

The female G-spot, named after Dr. Ernst Grafenberg, a German obstetrician, may take some practice to locate, but most women would be happy to oblige (unlike some of their more sexually conservative male counterparts in the female's pursuit of the male G-spot). While the woman lies on her back, the man should insert two fingers, pads facing up, into the vagina and then curl them back, applying firm, constant pressure to the upper vaginal wall. He can be assured that she will let him know when the massage feels good.

G-spot stimulation, alone or in conjunction with clitoral stimulation, may result in an orgasm so intense that a woman might feel a need to urinate. And many women claim to have actually "ejaculated" a clear, watery substance at the time of orgasm, although no one knows exactly what this is.

Other female hot spots include breasts, and the sensitive skin of the neck, lower abdomen, and inner arms and thighs. Of course, the most consistently responsive erogenous zone of all, the clitoris, welcomes touch, friction, massage, and just about any combination you create with your fingertips, mouth, and tongue.

SLAPS AND TAPS

WHEN SEXUAL TENSION ELECTRIFIES THE AIR ON A SECOND OR THIRD DATE, or an old flame needs a new warm-up, a good set of hands will never fail you.

The age-old line, "Hey, let me give you a massage" works like gangbusters, especially if you have some pleasantly scented massage oil nearby.

A good, all over body massage loosens muscles, relieves stress, and heightens sensory awareness, all of which are essential to feeling in the mood.

Begin at the shoulders with soft to medium pressure techniques, depending on how tight your partner feels, gripping muscles with palms and using fingertips to gently rub out or loosen any knots. Slowly work your way down the arms all the way to the hands, applying small, circular motions with your fingertips to the palms and each individual finger.

When you make your way back to the torso, expand your horizons to the lower back, buttocks, and legs, varying your touches to include kneading, tapping, light touches, and friction. A few feathery brush strokes of the fingertips will definitely induce the right kind of shivers, particularly when you reach more sensitive areas like the inner thighs or abdomen.

Another popular area of massage involves the feet, and if you're really motivated, you can learn about reflexology, and stimulate pressure points on your partner's feet that correspond with different internal organs and other body parts.

Scalp massage and digital stimulation of the facial muscles also prove extremely relaxing and are great ways to bring you and your partner together.

oral reports

Great food is like great sex—the
more you have the more you want.

—*Gael Greene*

Mouths say a lot when they say nothing at all.

Lips purse, sneer, pucker, and pout. They curve into frowns and smiles, or come together purposefully to convey business, all business. When excited or alarmed, mouths stand agape, and if we're really excited or feeling a little randy, tongues may hang out the side and ever so slowly encircle the mouth.

Regardless of what we say, how we use our mouths sexually reveals key truths about our personalities, inhibitions, and desires.

Lip Locks

GREAT LOVERS KNOW THE VALUE OF THE KISS, the slow and deliberate coming together of lips, breaths, and tongues that can be even more intimate than sex itself.

Our kisses speak volumes about what we're thinking and feeling, communicating to our partners our fears, nervousness, excitement, and sizzling hot passions. (Sometimes they communicate other things, like the roasted garlic pasta we had for lunch.)

Knowing a few basics about smooching will prime you and your lips for some serious make-out sessions. So brush your teeth and tongue and let's begin.

Brush your teeth and tongue again, floss, and gargle with a minty fresh liquid if you have any bad habits like smoking, heavy coffee drinking, or eating too much peanut butter. Kissing is so much more pleasant and inviting when you and your partner have clean, sweet-smelling breath.

Soft, smooth lips also make for pleasurable lip locks, so freely apply some unscented or mildly scented lip balm whenever necessary.

At the moment of truth, when faces gradually collide, do not pucker your lips as if you just sucked a lemon. And do not open your lips as if you're about to eat a super-sized deli sandwich!

Lips should be smooth, moist, relaxed, and together when they first meet. After that point, lips may begin to part ever so slightly at first, then just enough to let the tip of the tongue gently, slowly venture forth into your partner's mouth. Depending on your partner's response, you may choose to withdraw your tongue and focus instead on using your lips to kiss and caress other parts of the face, neck, and body. Not everyone loves tongue kissing.

But most people do, so when your partner's responses match your own, you may comfortably open your mouth wider and allow your tongue the freedom to explore (not deep sea dive). This kind of French kissing really stokes fires down below and serves as an enticing prelude to sex.

A word about hickeys: Don't.

Sexual relations should not leave physical bruises, scars, or marks of any kind. Consider the hickey an unwelcome relative of the kiss, and avoid prolonged sucking (think: barnacle on rock) on any one area of the body.

EATING OUT

The biggest barrier to embracing the delightful sensations of mouth on vulva, or cunnilingus, is fear—usually felt by the owner of the vulva.

Fear of potentially embarrassing odors. Fear that a partner might find the activity unpleasant or laborious. Fear of letting go of inhibitions, tensions, and fear itself and just enjoying the ride.

These fears are normal, sometimes even for couples in long term committed relationships, and only when both partners communicate their feelings of fear or uncertainty can they find ways to persevere.

One easy solution leads us back to the shower. Or bath tub. Fears of rank natural odors get washed right down the soapy drain.

As for the other stuff, if you or your

partner simply can't find a comfort level with this or any other sexual activity, just say no thank you and move on.

But for the cunning linguists and those who love them, here are a few helpful tips:

💜 Find a comfortable position. A popular favorite is when the woman lies on her back with knees bent, and the partner camps out between her legs.

💜 Use the protection of a dental dam, or good old-fashioned plastic wrap, if you're not 100 percent certain your partner is disease free.

💜 Always proceed slowly and gently.

💜 Vary your touches to include kisses, licks, flicks, and rubs. When she's ready, simultaneously stimulate her G-spot.

💜 Read her body language. Writhing,

arching the back, and tightening muscles in the buttocks are really good signs. Keep doing exactly what you're doing.

💜 Breathe, but never intentionally blow air into the vagina, which can cause serious damage.

💜 Don't whistle while you work. Hum.

💜 Better yet, add sensations with a vibrator.

💜 When in doubt, ask her what feels good. If she won't tell you, ask her to show you.

💜 Never forget that HIV and some other nasty germs may be transmitted through blood and body secretions, so always take precautions to keep you and your partner safe and healthy.

PLAYING THE FLUTE

THE BIGGEST BARRIER TO EMBRACING THE DELIGHTFUL SENSATIONS OF MOUTH ON PENIS, or fellatio, is fear—but definitely not felt by the owner of the penis.

Herein lies a key difference between the sexes. Whereas women may bashfully decline cunnilingus for all of the aforementioned reasons, men will never decline fellatio. Even if they're not springtime fresh. Even if they're feeling particularly shy, nervous, or tense. And even if they don't exactly know their partner, or care why she or he is missing several teeth.

In fact, the day a man declines a blow job may well be the day he's declared legally insane.

So ultimately, the key to a man's enjoyment of oral pleasure depends entirely on his ability to convince someone to do it.

One really good  way is for a man to first perform oral sex on his partner—with love, tenderness, and patience. When the tide turns, the man should be wary of appearing too forceful or demanding of reciprocation; rather, the penis should be offered as if presenting a gift to the gods (or goddesses, for that matter). Once accepted, the man should avoid any actions that involve excessive thrusting or the powerful manipulation of his partner's head. Last, he should always provide his partner the courtesy of knowing when he's about to ejaculate, so she can decide how best to handle the semen's arrival.

As for the art of performing fellatio, one can consult any number of serious sex manuals, such as the age-old Kama Sutra, which describes eight different techniques for "mouth congress" including "Sucking a Mango Fruit" and "Swallowing It Up."

You may also consider the following suggestions:

💜 Don't hesitate to hit the shower together as a prelude to oral sex. After all, cleanliness is next to godliness, and godliness means lots of oral sex.

💜 Use the protection of a condom—non-lubricated and flavored if possible—if you're not 100 percent certain your partner is disease free.

💜 Find a comfortable position. Favorites include: the man on his back with knees bent and the partner kneeling between his legs; or, both parties kneeling, with the man's torso straight and his partner's bent forward.

💜 Before mouth meets skin, fondle the penis and scrotum and tantalize with steamy hot breaths.

💜 Use your tongue to tickle and lick the entire penis, paying special attention to the head and frenulum.

💜 Keep him well lubricated with saliva by wrapping lips around his penis and doing a few head bobs.

💜 Keep your hands in the action by massaging his penis and scrotum or applying pressure at the base of the penis while you lick, bob, and suck.

💜 If he's receptive to the idea, try stimulating his G-spot while performing oral sex.

💜 Extend his pleasure by varying the speed and pressure of your touches.

💜 Remember that the average man ejaculates only 1-2 teaspoons at a time (or less than 40 calories worth).

💜 Also remember that HIV and some other nasty germs may be transmitted through

blood and body secretions, so always take precautions to keep you and your partner safe and healthy.

Final words on oral sex:

💜 Some couples find the 69 position, where the man (the 6) performs cunnilingus at the same time the woman (the 9) performs fellatio, to be a mutual turn-on which leads straight to intercourse. However, if you find it difficult to concentrate on your partner's pleasure while experiencing your own ecstasy, you may find it more fulfilling to "take turns."

💜 Even though it's called a "blow job," there's no blowing (or biting) involved.

♥ Remember the gag reflex before you deep throat up your lunch.

♥ Experimentation is the mother of sensation, so have some fun stimulating your partner using ice and heat, tasty lubricants and other edibles, and things that go buzz (but definitely not bees or wasps).

sex, sex, and more sex

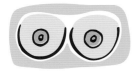

To succeed with the opposite sex,
tell her you're impotent.
She can't wait to disprove it.

—*Cary Grant*

Sexual intercourse strips us naked in more ways than one.

Personal and professional titles slip off with our underwear, and perceptions of who we are fade into realizations about what we are: hungry, passionate, intensely human animals.

Bodies, hot with desire, heave breathlessly as they connect, gasping and moaning with the relief and mind-numbing pleasure that penetration brings.

Every new position delivers different sensations that send tingles from head to toe, culminating at last in a glorious eruption of orgasmic release.

Sometimes we get so caught up in the heat of the moment that we become contortionist marathoners, wrenching our bodies (and especially our backs) into otherwise painful positions and keeping them there for way too long. Why? Because it hurts so good.

When the fog lifts and we emerge from our sex-induced haze, life returns to normal—but not really.

Back in his cubicle at the bank, the peon gofer recalls his inner dominator, and finally takes a stand, saying "I will only make three pots of coffee today." Meanwhile, the bank president gazes dreamily out her office window, unsure of exactly how she ended up straddling her masseur on his table at the spa, but certain she relished every minute of it.

Sex is all about discovering and embracing the passions that drive us and show us, for better or worse, who we really are.

And when we accept our very human cravings, filtering out the confusion and guilt that religion, culture, and "propriety" often bring, we can live life, give love, and prosper as nature intended.

THE HORIZONTAL HULA AND OTHER MOVES AND SHAKES

Sexual positions are as individual as tastes, and, like tastes, vary according to moods, physical cravings, and levels of excitement.

Any position that works for you is the right one, and innumerable possible combinations exist. The following popular standards can be slightly varied or radically transformed to make you and your partner  squeal with delight. Keep in mind that these are only a sampling of the limitless positions you can explore.

Man on Top (Missionary Position)

COMMENTS: A comfortable standby that is definitely not for missionaries only.

TECHNIQUE: The woman lies on her back with legs spread, raising her hips to meet her partner, while the man thrusts from a kneeling position.

FEMALE VARIATIONS: The woman bends her knees, folds them under or around her partner, or extends them straight out in a wide V. She can also rest knees or feet on her partner's shoulders. Adjusting leg position varies the degree of clitoral stimulation and depth of penetration.

MALE VARIATIONS: A man supports his body by resting on either side of the woman's body on his hands or forearms, or directly on her arms, knees, or thighs. He can also lie prostrate on top of the woman, creating friction that stimulates both partners.

Sex from Behind
(Doggie Style)

COMMENTS: This favorite for deep penetration and heavy thrusting may leave you both howling.

TECHNIQUE: The woman supports her body on hands and knees, while the man enters from behind, usually from the kneeling position.

FEMALE VARIATIONS: The woman extends her arms forward, resting her face and chest on the bed to change the angle of penetration. She can also lie flat on her stomach with legs spread.

MALE VARIATIONS: The man steadies himself by grasping the woman's shoulders or buttocks. He can also reach around and stimulate her breasts or vulva during penetration. With the woman pulled to the edge of the bed, he can thrust freely from a standing position.

Woman on Top
(Ride 'em Cowgirl)

COMMENTS: Allows females to control the thrusting, speed, and depth of penetration, and to vary clitoral stimulation. Yee haw!

TECHNIQUE: The man lies flat on his back while the woman, facing him, straddles his hips, taking his penis inside her as she lies flat on top of him.

FEMALE VARIATIONS: The woman stays in a kneeling position, and either faces toward or away from her partner. She can also reach underneath and fondle the man's scrotum and base of penis to add more stimulation.

MALE VARIATIONS: The man raises his hips to meet the woman, and stimulates her clitoris while she thrusts.

Side by Side
(Spoons)

COMMENTS: Great for lazy days and sleepy nights.

TECHNIQUE: The man enters the woman from behind as they lie side by side facing in the same direction.

FEMALE VARIATIONS: The woman bends one knee and lifts her leg in the air, allowing for deeper penetration. She can also roll onto her back with one leg raised and the man can straddle her other leg during penetration.

MALE VARIATIONS: The man can wrap one leg around the woman's leg, buttocks, or hip, depending on how flexible he is. He can also reach around with one hand and stimulate her vulva.

Standing
(The Elevator Shuffle)

COMMENTS: For adventurous spirits only.

TECHNIQUE: Both partners stand facing one another, achieving penetration by adjusting either partner's height so genitals match (e.g., standing on books, stairs, chairs).

FEMALE VARIATIONS: The woman lifts one leg, bending at the knee, and wraps it around the man's waist. She can also face away from her partner and bend at the waist, or, if she's really agile, she can stand on her hands while her partner supports her hips, thrusting between her legs.

MALE VARIATIONS: If he's physically able, the man can lift the woman's body and support her weight while she wraps both legs around his waist.

Sitting
(Lap Dancing)

COMMENTS: Good, bouncy, sexy fun.

TECHNIQUE: The man sits on a chair while the woman, facing him, straddles his lap and takes his penis inside her.

FEMALE VARIATIONS: The woman can extend both legs to the ground and control the thrusts from a modified standing position. Or, she can face away from her partner, adjusting her body to control the angle of penetration.

MALE VARIATIONS: The man can thrust upward while grasping his partner's buttocks, moving them in sync with his thrusts; or, he may sit back and allow the woman to control the action.

Spin Cycles, Kitchen Tables, Nooners, and Quickies

The thrill of sex soars to new heights when both partners actively seek ways to make it spontaneous, exciting, and new.

Titillate your partner with the element of surprise, appearing primed and ready for action when he or she least expects it—while he's doing the laundry, when she's washing her hair.

Initiate sexual encounters in new places, like the dining room, kitchen, locker room, or office conference room (after hours, of course).

Many couples experience heightened arousal when they run the risk of being caught in the act, which leads them to couple in public places like parking lots, stairwells, and outdoor parks or beaches. They may delight in this conspicuous lovemaking, but they certainly won't appreciate being charged with public indecency or exposure should they get caught.

And while the frenetically hurried, passionate sex of quickies might be over and done in the blink of an eye, the thrill and pleasure can keep you glowing all day long.

However and wherever you get it on (and in, up, and over), your sex life will never be dull when you keep your partner guessing about what you'll do next.

enjoying the ride

An intellectual is someone
who has found something more
interesting than sex.

—*Edgar Wallace*

Whenever we take up a new hobby, we devour every piece of information we can get our hands on.

Be it knitting, cycling, or cooking, we read the books. We buy the gadgets and the gizmos. We spend hours learning what to avoid and how best to perfect our skills.

Even so, sometimes we stumble. We poke ourselves with the knitting needle, fall off our bikes, or burn the chicken pot pie. But we chalk it up to experience and next time around, apply all that we have learned.

Taking this same approach with sex puts you in control of what is certain to become a lifelong hobby. And knowing the facts, especially regarding must-have gadgets and gizmos, can make all the difference.

SEXERCISE

The first time most people hear about Kegel exercises occurs after someone has had a baby.

Fearing the loss of bladder control or being too "loose" for their partners, and heeding doctors' advice, many women exercise their pubococcygeal (PC) muscles by squeezing the same muscles that stop and start the flow of urine. They flex and hold their PC muscles while standing in line at the grocery store, pitching ad campaigns, or addressing members of the United States Congress.

And their reward for doing these discreet exercises comes in the form of tight, fit vaginas that can actually grip a man's penis during sex, providing added sensation for both partners. Of course, women also regain any bladder control they may have lost during pregnancy.

Although Kegel exercises are designed for women, men can enjoy sexual benefits from performing them as well. If they add PC squeezes to their repertoires at the gym, they become more in tune with their bodies, leading them to better understand the sensations that immediately precede ejaculation. For men who experience premature ejaculation, Kegel exercises can be a godsend. But since the penis moves slightly (but noticeably) while men do Kegels, they might prefer "working out" in the privacy of their own homes.

LUBES AND TUBES

MOST OF THE TIME, NATURE PROVIDES ALL THE LUBRICATION WE NEED. Saliva and other slippery secretions enable penises to glide in and out of vaginas with pleasurable ease.

But sometimes, nature's juices get wiped away long before desire wanes. Wells run dry for other reasons too, such as stage of life, time of the month, stress, or side effects of common medications like antihistamines. When you use condoms, sex toys, and hands, and when sexual activities last a long time or take you to new and exciting places, good lubrication plays an essential role.

Knowing the pros and cons of the different over-the-counter lubricants will undoubtedly keep you safe and very, very satisfied.

For vaginal intercourse, water-based lubricants work the best. They are condom-safe, non-irritating or staining, and good enough to eat. Apply them liberally during sex whenever you want extra slippery satisfaction.

The only drawback to water-based lubes is that they contain a sugary substance called glycerin, and women prone to yeast infections may find that glycerin-free lubes work better for them.

Using any other type of lubricant in the vagina can be tricky. Just a smidgen of a silicone-based lubricant will provide unbelievable condom-safe slickness that seemingly lasts forever, but because silicone cannot be absorbed by the skin, clean-up becomes a real problem. Silicone lube can also interact with and damage silicone toys.

However, when it comes to anal sex, silicone lubes may be the all-around favorite, as they work uncommonly well and any residual lubricant gets eliminated naturally. Silicone lubes also make great massage gels, and can be wiped away with a little soap and water. Many other thick or gel lubricants specially designed for sex (not the doctor's office) are available and work well for anal play and masturbation.

Oil-based lubes destroy condoms and invite infection into the very sensitive vagina. Regardless of how desperate your situation, do not use petroleum jelly, Crisco, baby oil, or butter on a condom-covered penis or inside a vagina. If you happen to be male and all alone, though, use whatever looks most appealing at the moment—even if it happens to be applesauce.

REALLY FUN TOYS

Remember that favorite toy you played with as a kid? You spent hours touching it, talking to it, even sleeping with it. You couldn't imagine life without it.

Well, although the toys have changed, those feelings of attachment to a toy may never end.

And thanks to the Internet, you don't even have to risk being seen entering one of those stores to find a toy that's right for you (although instant retail gratification has its own rewards).

In fact, suburban housewives have put the Tupperware parties on hold because there's a new game in town—sex toy parties. You can choose from a wide array of "bedroom accessories" and novelty items in the comfort of someone's living room. What better way to buy the penis ice cube trays and super-sized dildo you had on your Christmas list?

Let's be honest here. Everyone knows that the vibrating "massage" wand you bought at the mall won't really be used on your back. Why not learn what's out there and get what you truly want.

The following toy categories will give you a general idea of the kind of fun you might be missing.

VIBRATORS come in all shapes and sizes and add pleasurable sensations to nearly every male and female body part. Choose from vibrating underwear to thimble-like vibes that fit on fingers, or the very popular "Rabbit" styles that stimulate several areas at once. For many people, it's "love at first vibrate" no matter what style you choose, because orgasms are virtually impossible to prevent.

DILDOS resemble penises, though some have more realistic sizes and textures than others. They can be worn with a harness or mounted on a shower wall, and enjoyed by men and women alike. Some dildos even fit mini vibrators inside, so you can stimulate your partner or yourself in more ways than one.

MASTURBATION SLEEVES, also known as "pocket pussies," resemble vaginas in feel and texture, especially when made from some of the life-like materials now available. Men can experience similar sensations to intercourse with a sleeve, especially when used with a compatible lubricant.

PLUGS AND BEADS are for assholes only (just kidding). These sex toys fit inside the anus and may be used in combination with genital stimulation or intercourse. While butt plugs are inserted into the anus and stay put, anal beads, which resemble a loosely spaced string of marble-sized beads, are inserted into the anus and, during orgasm, slowly pulled out to create new dimensions of sexual pleasure.

PUMPS AND RINGS are tools that help men get it up and keep it up. Penis pumps fit over penises creating suction that helps men achieve erections. They swell blood vessels that temporarily enlarge the penis, but do not have lasting effects. Cock rings are rings usually made of metal, rubber, or leather that slide over the penis and fit snugly at the base, restricting blood flow to prolong or enhance an erection. Cock rings come in assorted colors and styles, including ones with pleasure nubs to stimulate the clitoris during intercourse.

protective gear

Somewhere on this globe,
every ten seconds, there is a woman
giving birth to a child. She must
be found and stopped.

—*Sam Levenson*

Ignorance may be blissful, but in matters of sex, it can also be inconvenient, unpleasant, or deadly.

HERE ARE THE FACTS:

🖤 Women get sexually transmitted diseases (STDs) much more easily than men, due to basic physiology.

🖤 Women get pregnant when eggs come in contact with sperm, and this can happen through sexual play as well as intercourse.

🖤 The only sure protection against HIV and other STDs is abstinence or the use of condoms.

Having safe sex with must-have, no-excuses accessories keeps it fun—and it might just save your life.

Rubber Raincoats

Thanks to science and technology, we can have our partners and eat them too—safely.

Latex and polyurethane products for men and women create physical barriers that prevent sperm and tiny viruses from entering bodies. People who aren't 100 percent certain their partners are disease-free can keep themselves protected by regular, proper use of products made from these materials.

Products made of lambskin, or more accurately, lamb intestines, do provide adequate birth control but do not protect against HIV and tiny viruses.

Male condoms come in various sizes, textures, colors, and flavors, and are usually prepackaged with spermicidal lubricant, though not always. They resemble thin, elastic socks that fit over the penis, fitting roomy at the head and snug at the base of the penis.

Although any barrier placed over the highly sensitive penis will dull sensation a bit, many brands of condoms succeed in maximizing sensation in the right areas. Latex condoms tend to be the most popular choice for many couples, due to their high elasticity, ready availability, and low cost. Partners can have some serious fun experimenting with different brands and styles until they find one they like best. The only downside to latex concerns heat, as higher temperatures will weaken latex products until they break. So keep latex condoms out of the sunshine and put on a new one if sex lasts a long time.

People with latex allergies will find close alternatives in polyurethane condoms, although polyurethane is somewhat less elastic than latex and experiences more breakage.

Female condoms are wide tubes of latex or polyurethane, with one closed end fitting inside the vagina over the cervix, and a larger end staying outside the body. Unlike a male condom, female condoms do not hug the penis; rather, they line the interior of the vagina to prevent viruses, germs, and sperm from getting in. Female condoms are an absolute necessity if, for whatever reason, the man is not wearing a condom. In order for them to work, however, they must be used alone (not in conjunction with a male condom) and properly throughout the duration of intercourse.

Dental dams are latex or polyurethane sheaths designed specifically for oral sex activities on vulvas or anuses. They serve as excellent protection against viruses and germs, but do, unfortunately, dull sensation. For this reason, some people rely on regular plastic wrap— although not the kind made for microwaves

because it has microscopic holes that can be penetrated by HIV and other tiny viruses.

Latex or polyurethane gloves may also come in handy depending on where your fists and fingers find themselves.

Top 10 Reasons to Use Condoms

HIV

SYPHILIS

GONORRHEA

HEPATITIS

HERPES

CHLAMYDIA

CRABS

GENITAL WARTS

3 A.M. FEEDINGS

AIDS

THERE FOR THE PICKIN'

HAVING SEX MAKES BABIES, and babies, although cuddly and cute, are a lot of work. Before you and your partner decide to get pregnant, spend a long weekend babysitting someone else's three young children. The sleep deprivation, maniacal pace, and constant demands may well leave you and your partner running straight to the gynecologist's office for some birth control.

Women soon discover that, although men play an equal role in the making of babies, women alone bear the weight of responsibility when it comes to contraception. Aside from male condoms or surgical sterilization, most birth control options are specifically designed for women, making it critical for them to get educated and take action. And because the decision affects her body, a woman should ultimately decide what's right for her—preferably a choice that works equally well for her partner.

The best approach to contraception involves a visit to the gynecologist, which the woman may do with or without her partner. There, she can learn about the pros and cons of the many different options available, including the following list of possibilities:

THE PATCH—a small adhesive patch a woman can wear on her body for a week at a time that delivers contraceptive hormones absorbed through the skin.

THE PILL—a daily, oral dose of contraceptive hormones a woman ingests every day.

INTRAUTERINE DEVICE (IUD)—a plastic device fitted into a woman's uterus by a doctor and kept in place for years at a time.

INJECTIONS—contraceptive hormones injected through the skin by a doctor. They can last for three months at a time.

VAGINAL RING—a circular device inserted in

a woman's cervix each month that delivers contraceptive hormones absorbed by her body.

FEMALE CONDOM—a tubular latex or polyurethane device that slides into the vagina, creating a safe pathway for intercourse.

SPERMICIDE—sperm-killing foam, jelly, cream, or suppository that can be inserted into the vagina prior to intercourse.

DIAPHRAGM—a rubbery cap fitted to a woman's cervix that a woman inserts into her vagina prior to intercourse. Must be used with spermicide.

CERVICAL CAP—a thimble-shaped cap fitted to a woman's cervix that a woman inserts into her vagina prior to intercourse. Must be used with spermicide.

SURGERY—permanent and irreversible sterilization achieved by tying a woman's fallopian tubes in knots, or removing the internal female reproductive organs.

kinking it up a notch

There are a number of
mechanical devices which increase
sexual arousal, particularly in
women. Chief among these is the
Mercedes-Benz 380SL convertible.

—*P. J. O'Rourke*

Like spiking your drink with an extra shot of vodka, or spicing up the chili with just one more jalapeño pepper, some activities intensify sensations and bump sex to a higher plane.

Ordinary sex can become extraordinary when you brave new physical, psychological, and spiritual territories. Remember how much you loved riding that roller coaster, despite your initial fears and hesitation? Or what about that time you bungee-jumped off that bridge, experiencing the biggest, most intense thrill of your life?

When you embrace your inner explorer and connect with your partner in new and exciting ways, sex can be anything but routine.

BUMMING AROUND

ANUSES HAVE LONG BEEN STIGMATIZED AS DIRTY, UNTOUCHABLE ONE-WAY CHUTES DESIGNED FOR ONE THING ONLY: ELIMINATION. Fears, myths, and misunderstandings about anal sex and anal play cause unnecessary homophobic preoccupations in many people.

But the real dirt on the butt reveals what some men and women already know: that this "other" hole can be a sexual playground. Like its genital neighbors, the anus swells with blood during sexual arousal, becoming highly attuned to sensation. The slightest touch on the rim of the anus may heighten sexual pleasure, while actual penetration by a lubricated toy or body part may create intense full body orgasms.

Before you go knocking on anyone's back door, or before you open yours to your best friend, it's important to take care of some necessary business.

As with any sexual activity, good hygiene makes for pleasant coupling. If you think your evening might include some anal play, use a little extra soap and water on your anus while you're in the shower.

Stock up on condoms and lubricant, and be sure to put condoms on any sex toys that might visit the back forty. To that end, sex toys and/or body parts that plan to visit several areas during one extended trip (say, anuses, vaginas, and mouths) must always, always, always be washed thoroughly beforehand. In fact, the best idea involves purchasing specific toys for specific activities, and only using them as such. Since women are especially prone to urinary tract infections, their partners should never go from touching anuses to vulvas without first washing up.

When it comes to anal intercourse, people may find the experience far from painful.

With trust between partners, relaxation, and, of course, plenty of lubricant, anal penetration can be a deeply pleasurable means of expressing love and affection.

Some final thoughts to clear the air surrounding the butt: anal play and intercourse are not just homosexual activities. Not all gay people enjoy these practices, and the heterosexuals who do are not secretly gay, deviant, or perverted. They might simply be you, a few weeks from now. But great care and caution come with the territory, because the skin inside the rectum is tender and easily abraded, making the transmission of HIV especially easy when condoms and lubricant aren't used.

KINK AND FANTASY PLAY

PLAYING MAKE-BELIEVE TRANSPORTS US TO MAGICAL LANDS WHERE DREAMS CAN COME TRUE. Fairy princesses wave leather whips, not wands, and princes wear satin and lace.

Sometimes, the sharing of erotic fantasies can lead to increased intimacy in a relationship, allowing you and your partner the freedom to experiment, play, and explore. Other times, it's best to keep your fantasies to yourself, particularly if they involve woolly farm animals or your boyfriend's brother.

Sigmund Freud famously said, "When two people make love, there are at least four people present—the two who are actually there and the two they are thinking about." Add to that the two they are pretending to be, and the bed gets mighty crowded.

But, with a few exceptions, mind games and role playing in the bedroom can be an exciting part of a healthy, active relationship—especially one that is characterized by good communication, understanding, and respect. These qualities become absolutely essential when one partner has control over another in sexual power play, such as sadomasochism (S/M), bondage and discipline (B/D), and dominance and submission (D/S). Establishing rules of engagement and having a safe word to let your partner know when you've had enough (e.g., "Macaroni") ensures that the game will end when you want it to. It's also important to use gentle toys for your erotic play (e.g., furry handcuffs, soft blindfold), so no one leaves the game with a physical reminder.

Major kink! Some scientists believe that the male praying mantis can copulate successfully only when half his head has been eaten off.

Mild kink might include having a sexual fetish, or getting uncommonly aroused by a certain object or body part. People with leather fetishes, for example, might need to touch and smell leather in order to climax. Cross-dressers like to dress up as members of the opposite sex, although oftentimes they lead very ordinary, heterosexual lives. Other kinky stuff like exhibitionism (think: showing your stuff in public) and voyeurism (think: peeping at other people's stuff) can get you into trouble with the law in most states, unless, of course, you're performing for or peeping at your partner.

THE TANTRIC ZONE

WHEN CHOCOLATE LOVERS VISIT the chocolate factory in Hershey, Pennsylvania, they have Tantric sex with chocolate (for all intents and purposes). They fall into a sort of meditative trance—a chocolate stupor, if you will—gazing blissfully at huge vats of melted chocolate, deeply inhaling the sweet chocolate air, feeling a pleasure they wish would last forever.

Now, if you're a chocolate lover and your partner happens to be covered in chocolate, you just might have reached nirvana.

Followers of Tantra practice synchronized deep breathing techniques, steady eye contact, and yoga-like meditation to extend sensual pleasures and connect with sexual and spiritual energies. Tantric sex sessions can last for hours (or at least, that's what the musician Sting says), allowing partners to focus on all over body sensations that intensify sexual pleasure without focusing on orgasm.

If you wish to imbue the Tantric spirit in your bedroom, you should devote at least five hours to the activity, practicing motionless sex, breathing in sync with your partner, and, most important, listening to your favorite Sting songs over and over again.

flying solo

Don't knock masturbation.
It's sex with someone I love.

—*Woody Allen*

Sometimes you just have to take matters into your own hands.

And why not? Why does the rooster crow? Why do kangaroos hop? Why do dogs lick themselves? Because they can.

And so can we (especially during the Masturbate-A-Thon every May when you can "come for a cause").

Masturbation is as natural as sunshine in the desert, as refreshing as the Nestea plunge. And it's true what they say: sex is always good with the one you love, particularly when that person is you.

GETTING YOUR PALM RED

Forget about the teddy bears and toy rattles, the trucks and balls and mitts: the first toy men ever received still gets all the play.

It gets polished and stroked, and sometimes choked, flogged, and spanked—all in the name of pleasure. Guilty pleasure, that is.

At a relatively early age, men discovered that masturbation doesn't cause blindness, and that penises rarely break (although they can be injured if they bend during sex). They perfected the art of touching themselves, and practiced and practiced until things were made . . . perfect. Most important, they found that they were not alone (in one sense, at least), realizing that legions of men before them had done exactly the same things.

Maybe just not with vacuum cleaner hoses, or their sisters' silky nightgowns, or while thinking about movie stars and nearly everyone they ever knew.

And that could be why men still feel some sense of guilt when they masturbate.

TEASING THE LITTLE MAN IN THE CANOE

The art of female masturbation is as easy as riding a bike.

And believe it or not, that's how many young girls begin to notice certain sensations down below. Activities like horseback riding take those feelings to new heights, and then, if they're lucky, they stumble upon their mother's "back massager" and life never looks the same.

Like boys, girls discover at an early age that touching themselves a certain way feels good. As adults, many women still want and need extra touches during intercourse, because, unlike men, intercourse alone does not usually stimulate their clitorises. To have an orgasm, they need their pearls polished.

This anatomical fact requires both men

and women to confront masturbation, look him straight in the face, and extend a welcoming hand. Women who communicate to their partners what feels good, where they like to be touched, and how best to do it, tend to be the most satisfied.

Then again, when she's all alone, she and masturbation can have their own little secrets.

Online Lovin'

Getting off while you're online is so easy nowadays.

Enter just about any word in any search engine and, voilà, up pops a slew of X-rated websites you can visit in the blink of a mouse click. And thousands of chat rooms encourage tantalizing e-mail correspondence with seemingly gorgeous, appealing, lonely models.

Unfortunately, many of these models you know so well through e-mail turn out to be middle-aged, obese shut-ins or, worse yet, predatory, sick people hoping to dupe you into meeting in person.

Luckily, since you're smart, you won't fall for any online trickery. But, if you're excessively horny, you should be cautioned about spending too much time pursuing "harmless" online titillation—especially if you're in a committed relationship.

Because too much of anything—caffeine, bon bons, masturbation—detracts from what's really important in life, and hopefully, you've discovered that this means making healthy, positive connections with others face to face.

coming over obstacles

It is not enough to conquer;
one must know how to seduce.

—*Voltaire*

Sometimes, having sex just ain't so easy.

What should be beautiful, magical, and rewarding is instead fraught with frustrations, interruptions, or physical challenges.

Understanding some very common obstacles may help you triumph in the bedroom, regardless of whether or not intercourse takes place.

BUN IN THE OVEN

Surveys reveal that married people have the most sex.

Until, of course, the woman gets pregnant and her body swells to unrecognizable proportions, making the act somewhat less appealing for some and logistically difficult for others.

He may love her pregnant body even more, but she might worry about what the baby can see, hear, and feel. And everyone will know what bad parents you are when baby emerges from the womb with a penis-indented head.

Managing through the myriad changes that pregnancy brings to a relationship will ultimately strengthen the bonds between you and your partner. Doctors advise people to continue having normal sexual relations during pregnancy; as long as things feel good, there's no reason to stop. When labor doesn't progress at the end of the ninth month, some couples are actually encouraged to have inter-course, because the prostaglandins in semen may get things started naturally.

You and your partner will need to decide what's right for you during pregnancy, and that might mean finding creative new posi-tions that make you scream "Mama," or sim-ply cuddling by a warm fire picking out baby names. As always, though, it's important to pay close attention to your body and practice safe sex, so everyone stays happy and healthy.

KIDS IN THE HOUSE

Men learn very quickly that father-hood requires a lot of patience—of the saint variety.

 After a woman gives birth, her body needs time to heal, especially if she's had a caesarean section or episiotomy (think: slice through the perineum). Physical healing can take weeks and often months, and even then she may be less than enthusiastic about getting down and dirty in the sack. She's a mother now.

And she's really, really, really tired—especially if she's breastfeeding. So while he's dreaming about blow jobs and bending her over a chair, she's pining for sleep. At the same time, she's busy changing diapers, nursing or bathing the baby, going to doctor's appointments, doing endless piles of laundry, and, very often, working outside the home.

To quell the surging feelings of resentment that naturally build and are fueled by her fluctuating hormones, the man must tread very, very lightly if he ever hopes to have sex with her again in his natural lifetime. This means helping her in every way imaginable, surprising her "just because," and reminding her in every way that she's beautiful, sexy, and most of all, a great mother. If all else fails, leave the baby with grandma and check into a hotel. Nothing rekindles old flames like stale hotel air and dirty movies on cable TV.

When the fog of new parenthood lifts and kids are old enough to open doors, the best aphrodisiac for the whole family comes in the form of . . . Sponge Bob Square Pants. Actually, any cartoon will do. Parents of older children recognize the value of 30-minute

television programs that keep their kids engaged—and smart ones seize opportunities when they arise, even if just for a quickie in the next room.

Sex will never be what it was before kids ran your life (at least until they grow up and leave the house), but it can be just as enjoyable. Sometimes even more so, because with greater challenges lie greater rewards.

SAHARAS, SOFTIES, AND STDS

Most sexual problems are easy to treat, if only people would get themselves to a doctor and open their mouths. Instead, they suffer in silence and avoid embarrassing situations.

Granted, confronting your own problems can be difficult enough, let alone sharing them with a doctor or therapist. But finding the courage to take that necessary first step will lead you toward a treatment that's right for you.

Some of the most common sexual problems include erectile dysfunction, premature ejaculation, vaginal dryness, and sexually transmitted diseases (STDs).

Depending upon the exact type of your erectile difficulties, treatment may involve medication, exercises, smoking cessation, or psychotherapy. All men experience some degree of erectile dysfunction at some point in their lives, especially when suffering great anxiety or stress. But knowing this may be of little help to the man who can't get or sustain an erection. These days, the prescription drug Viagra and newer copycat drugs are widely used to help men achieve and maintain erections.

For older men, who experience impotence more frequently than younger men, solutions may also involve changing the timing of sexual activities (e.g., first thing in the morning), or seeking other medical solutions such as penile implants or injections. Another device called a vacuum pump temporarily "pumps" up the penis to create an erection, but side effects may include bruising and difficulty ejaculating.

Premature ejaculation describes a condition in which men ejaculate before they (or their partners) are ready. Since "readiness" is subjective, this might mean after 20 minutes of sexual intercourse for one man or, for another, before it ever begins. Several techniques may remedy ejaculatory control issues, but the "stop-start" technique developed by Dr. James Semans in 1955 usually proves to be the most successful. This approach focuses the man's attention on premonitory sensations, the sensations that indicate his point of no return. As the man becomes increasingly aroused, he is advised to practice "stopping" at each level of arousal, allowing himself to calm down to a pre-aroused state before "starting" all over again.

Many women experience vaginal dryness when estrogen levels fluctuate, which can occur at various times of the menstrual cycle, after giving birth, or after menopause. Left untreated, this condition can cause burning, irritation, and painful intercourse. Thankfully, the use of specially formulated personal lubricants can now restore vaginal lubrication and keep women feeling healthy and sexually active.

Many STDs simply disappear, with few (if any) visible scars, once they are treated with antibiotics or other prescription drugs The psychological scars, however, may last. But if you've contracted something more permanent, like HIV or genital warts, you can still enjoy a healthy, active sex life as long as you take precautions. Depending on your specific symptoms, wearing a condom or dental dam may be all it takes. For your partner's sake as well as your own, speak to your physician about safe sex practices and follow your doctor's advice at all times.

Whatever sex-related problem you face, be it erectile dysfunction, premature ejaculation, inability to reach orgasm, or infertility, both you and your partner can't go wrong by educating yourself and acting upon appropriate, available options.